WATCH THEM
•••••••
GROW!

The Life Cycle of a SUNFLOWER

Bonnie Phelps

PowerKiDS press

New York

Published in 2016 by The Rosen Publishing Group, Inc.
29 East 21st Street, New York, NY 10010

First Edition

Editor: Caitie McAneney
Book Design: Reann Nye

Photo Credits: Cover Maxim Petrichuk/Shutterstock.com; p. 5 Serp/Shutterstock.com; p. 6 ksena2you/ Shutterstock.com; p. 9 Yaromir/Shutterstock.com; pp. 10, 18, 23 (sprout), 24 (stem) Africa Studio/Shutterstock.com; p. 13 (background) amenic181/Shutterstock.com; p. 13 (background) amenic181/Shutterstock.com; pp. 13 (seed), 14 Filipe B. Varela/Shutterstock.com; pp. 17, 24 (soil, root) Richard Griffin/Shutterstock.com; p. 20 (bud) Pavelk/Shutterstock.com; pp. 20 (inset), 23 (flower) motodan/Shutterstock.com.

Library of Congress Cataloging-in-Publication Data

Phelps, Bonnie, author.
 The life cycle of a sunflower / Bonnie Phelps.
     pages cm. — (Watch them grow!)
 Includes bibliographical references and index.
 ISBN 978-1-4994-0684-9 (pbk.)
 ISBN 978-1-4994-0685-6 (6 pack)
 ISBN 978-1-4994-0686-3 (library binding)
 1. Sunflowers—Juvenile literature. 2. Sunflowers—Life cycles—Juvenile literature. I. Title. II. Series: Watch them grow!
 QK495.C74P49 2015
 583'.99—dc23
                        2014048540

Manufactured in the United States of America

CPSIA Compliance Information: Batch #WS15PK: For Further Information contact Rosen Publishing, New York, New York at 1-800-237-9932

Contents

Sunflowers are big and yellow. They can grow very tall!

A sunflower changes as it grows. These changes make up its life cycle.

A sunflower drops seeds from its flower. Can you see this sunflower's seeds?

seeds

A sunflower seed holds a baby plant inside. It also holds enough food to get the plant started.

A sunflower seed needs water and healthy **soil**. This helps it grow.

The plant inside the seed grows.
It breaks out of the seed's shell.

The baby plant is called a sprout. It grows **roots**. It also pushes up through the ground.

roots →

leaves

stem

A sprout grows a **stem** and leaves. Leaves use sunlight to make food.

Next, a bud starts to grow.
In time, the bud opens.

The sunflower grows into a tall adult plant. It drops seeds of its own. The life cycle begins again!

Life Cycle of a Sunflower

Words to Know

roots

soil

stem

Index

Websites

Due to the changing nature of Internet links, PowerKids Press has developed an online list of websites related to the subject of this book. This site is updated regularly. Please use this link to access the list: www.powerkidslinks.com/wtg/sun